Introduction

The Chadian government is in a fragile state because of a division of society over tribal ethnicity, political organizations with preferential policies, and consistent challenges from rebel groups. All of these internal matters present major dilemmas for Chadian citizens and regional governments. The Chadian government is not capable of addressing these problems alone. African institutions and the international community must address these problems with a coordinated strategy.[1]

As the 5th largest country in Africa, Chad's internal strife, regional disagreements, and international responses to these matters should not be overlooked and deserve consistent monitoring. Chad is a landlocked country roughly twice the size of Texas with a turbulent history of religious and ethnic conflict, including an intermittent civil war.[2] Bordered by Libya to the north and Sudan to the east, it is among the world's 10 poorest countries, according to the United Nations Development Program (UNDP) Human Development Index. Persistent conflicts have also hindered the country's development, despite significant oil reserves.[3]

Chad's instability derives from internal factors. Some attribute Chad's problems to external factors such as the Darfur crisis in Sudan, but the Darfur crisis alone only compounds Chad's instability. Chad's efforts to deal with political, security, and humanitarian problems have lacked coordination and has not gained enough attention to be a significant priority. There is a regional agreement that a comprehensive strategy encompassing the national, regional, and international dimensions of the crisis is required to move toward peace and stability both within Chad and between Chad and its neighbors.[4]

This study commences with an assessment of the current situation in Chad, which will provide background information on social, political, economic, and military matters. Regional

1

players also have a key role in Chadian affairs; therefore, analyzing Chad's interaction with neighboring countries will provide insight on Chadian relations in the region. Finally, this paper concludes with identifying the international response to matters in Chad and provides likely motives for outside interaction in Chadian affairs.

Through this case study, readers will increase their knowledge in Central African affairs and understand the current effects of an unstable Chadian government; additionally, readers will understand the role the international community plays in helping Chad become a stable and prosperous nation.

Chadian Internal Challenges

Social

Chad has over 200 ethnic groups. Northern and Eastern Chadians are by and large Muslim (50%), while most southerners are Christians (25%) or animists (25%). Over the course of lengthy religious and commercial relationships with neighboring Arab countries like Sudan and Egypt, many eastern and central Chadian regions "have become more or less Arabized."[5] Southern Chadians have taken to the European culture dating back to the French colonial period, contributing to the north-south division. The division between the north and south is the most significant source of conflict in Chad since its independence.

Historically, the French favored southern Chadians over northern Chadians, while neighboring Arab countries favored the northerners over the southerners.[6] The European administration intensified the feeling of ethnic separateness by drawing local boundaries along perceived ethnic lines.[7] This regional divide has increased feelings of bitterness and violence. The Europeans assigned chiefs and other local African authorities who had little legitimacy over the groups they were to lead, which in turn, destroyed southern organizations in favor of uniform chiefdoms.

The failure of European powers to establish indigenous leadership systems ignited cultural issues such as the lack of transparency, accountability, and democratic processes. Furthermore, deep-rooted ethnic splits confront the Chadian government's attempts to raise a united Chadian country. Due to unwise social systems that began during the French colonial period, Chad has continuously had to deal with ethnic bias.

During the French colonial occupation period, the Europeans failed to unify Chad and did very little to promote modernization of the country. In the French scale of priorities, the colony of Chad ranked near the bottom; it was less important than non-African territories, North Africa, West Africa, or even the other French possessions in Central Africa.[8] The French viewed Chad as simply a supply source for cotton and labor to aid colonies in the south. Lacking resources and the will to establish a basic rule of law for the country resulted in a lack of governance except in the south.

Political

The 1946 Chadian constitution declared Chad a French territory. Although Chadians participated in French politics, they insisted on additional political rights including training in administrative and technical areas to assist in establishing a Chadian run government with an independent Chadian political agenda. In the late 1950s, political shifts led to more internal influence on Chadian politics. Ultimately, a repressive regime contributed to Chad's fragmentation openly discriminating against northerners.[9]

Dissention in Chad led to increasing destabilization and created new dissidents. In 1975, political unrest in Chad led to a government coup, which resulted in the first insurgent Chadian President, Goukouni Oueddei (1979-1982), of the northern Toubou tribe. As neighboring Libyan leader Muammar Qadhafi gained power and influence in the region, he began to exploit Chad's instability by declaring a merger between Libya and Chad. He stationed military forces in northern Chad and channeled aid to Chadian insurgents at the request of President Oueddei.[10]

When a rival northern figure former Defense Minister, Hissein Habre (1982-1990), took control of the Chadian government, he asked Libyan forces in Chad to leave. Although the Chadian government had a new leader, Libyan influence to establish a Muslim leader remained. Expanding Libyan interests and reducing outside influence across Africa remained a priority.

In 1990, another Libyan backed leader from the north, Idriss Deby (1990-current) took control of the Chadian government. After stabilizing Chad, he was the first to have open elections in Chad. Deby won Chad's first election and was confirmed as President; however, opposition from a previous Chadian Defense Minister from the north, Youssouf Togoimi (1995-1997), resulted in an insurgency. In an effort to end the fighting, Libya brokered a peace treaty to declare a cease-fire in the region to end a three-year war; however, infighting in Togoimi's political party blocked the peace treaty from finalization.[11]

Violent clashes between the government and rebel groups appear to be a routine cycle in Chad. Chad's 1993 National Sovereign Conference served as the catalyst for Chad's democratic transition led by President Deby. Since the conference, there has been a steady rollback and disregard for democratic principles.[12] As a result, greater opposition to the Deby government has been prevalent and peace deals have been unsuccessful. The need for electoral reform and a demilitarized government remain to be issues in Chad, if not resolved, will continue the cycle of violence and government opposition.

Economic

France granted Chad independence in 1960 and Chad subsequently has depended heavily on foreign assistance. Chad's dependence on foreign aid keeps the Chadian government functional: finances debt incurred from trading, drought, and famine; and also rebuilds the country/government after combat operations. Initially, France was Chad's most viable economic aid provider.

From 1979 to early 1980, all foreign economic assistance to Chad ceased with the exception of France. The US, in particular, began economic ties with modest contributions, but halted assistance because the Chadian presidency, held by Goukouni Oueddei, was a supporter of and received support from Libya. The US restricted aid to Chad by sending only food and infrastructure assistance.

US aid increases to Chad did not occur until the 1980s. During this period, Chad saw a steady increase of support because the US recognized that Chadian instability threatened regional stability. The economic contributions not only aided in infrastructure, but included agreements on training programs to improve the efficiency of the Chadian government in an attempt to gain popular support and confidence from native Chadians.

Chad's economic potential mostly relates to the oil and gas industry. In 1969 the discovery of potentially recoverable oil reserves near Doba resulted from the US oil company Conoco. Conoco received rights from the Chadian government to explore 100 percent of Chad's oil fields, covering approximately twenty million acres.[13] With additional reserves discovered in 1975, the focus veered towards using the proceeds to fund Chad's domestic needs.

> By 1980, this field yielded approximately 1,500 barrels of oil per day. Major American oil corporations such as Chevron and ExxonMobil joined the consortium at this stage. However, deepening internal conflict and violence between the various factions led to the withdrawal of the consortium and the suspension of further oil exploration.[14]

Established in 1988, the oil consortium to explore in Chad permitted exploration until 2004.[15]

A 30-year concession was established to develop an oil field near Doba to produce and transport oil to markets via a pipeline. The pipeline cuts though Cameroon to the Atlantic Ocean and began producing oil in 2004. According to the United Institute of Peace (USIP), oil revenues have increased Chad's budget to grow fifty times the amount in 2004. The World Bank required the Chadian government to invest the oil revenues in development projects and priorities.[16] This guideline for Chad assisted the government in managing profits from oil revenue to avoid mismanagement of funds and resources.

In 2006, the World Bank's withdrawal from the project resulted in pipeline revenue being used to strengthen the military, leaving no money for infrastructure development. In 2009, Chad's military expenditures grew five times the budget amount in 2004.[17] The explanation for this huge military expenditure revolved around security for internal matters and the Darfur conflict.

Military

The Chadian Armed Forces was the first official Army of Chad, composed of mostly soldiers from Southern Chad.[18] The Army practiced French military traditions from World War I until 1979. In 1979, it lost its status because the civil and military administration disintegrated. The fighting force was reduced to a regional Army fighting for Southern interests. When Mr. Habre assumed the Chadian presidency in 1982, his Army became the core of Chad's military. In 1982, with assistance from the French, the Armed Forces of the North emerged victorious while fighting against forces loyal to Mr Oueddei. The Armed Forces of the North were officially constituted in January 1983, when the various pro-Habre contingents were merged and renamed FANT (Forces Army North Tchadiennes).[19]

In the mid-1980s, the US sent military specialists to Chad temporarily to train the Chadian military on equipment received from the US. From 1984 to 1987, US military aid to Chad totaled about US$70 million; an additional US$9 million was proposed for FY 1988.[20] A majority of the assistance included transport aircraft and aircraft maintenance, small arms, ammunition, trucks, jeeps, antiaircraft and antitank weapons, uniforms, first aid kits, and food rations.[21]

In 1989, Idriss Deby, a top military commander in the Chadian armed forces, revolted and fled to neighboring Sudan. When Mr. Deby revolted, soldiers loyal to him followed Mr.

Deby to Sudan. In 1990, Mr. Deby used soldiers to march into N'djamena, the capital city of Chad, to drive out President Habre. Among the forces supporting Deby were northern Muslims, Sudanese natives whom Mr. Deby recruited while in Sudan, as well as, a number of southerners.

At the end of Mr. Habre's regime, Chad's armed forces consisted of 36,000 troops, but grew to roughly 50,000 in the early stages under President Deby.[22] In 1991 though, the aim of reducing the size of the armed forces was supported by France and reorganization took place. An essential element of this effort was to make the ethnic composition of the armed forces reflective of the country as a whole.[23] This effort decreased the size of the military, but northerners held control of high ranking leadership positions.

Resistance from the south continued in the 1990s, as southern resistance groups initiated threats to oust President Deby from power. Either Chadian forces crushed the resistance or little to no progress surfaced. The Movement for Democracy and Justice in Tchad (MDJT) posed a threat which resulted in a formal peace accord. Although remnants of MDJT are still present in the North, active rebellion there has been negligible since late 2003.[24]

A major concern for Chadian defense continues to be the lengthy, permeable border of Chad. In March 2004, the Algerian terrorist organization, the Salafist Group for Preaching, and Combat (GSPC), strayed into Chadian territory, where they were engaged by Chadian armed forces.[25] Herein lays a continuous problem for a small Chadian force which lacks the appropriate personnel or equipment to deter such issues. This leaves Chad very susceptible to armed groups crossing the Chadian border resulting in more violence and instability in the region.

Chadian Regional Relations

Chad currently has no official relationship with France, its former colonial power, although it continues to receive economic assistance from the European Union, the United States, and various international organizations such as the Swiss Agency for Development and Cooperation (SDC), World Vision, and World Food Program. Libya is a major provider to Chad and has a resident ambassador in N'Djamena, the capital city. Other resident diplomatic missions in N'Djamena include the embassies of France, the United States, Egypt, Algeria, Iraq, Sudan, Germany, the Central African Republic, Zaire, Nigeria, China, Cameroon, and the European Economic Community.[26] There are also numerous countries with non-resident ambassadors due to concurrent obligations in other African countries. Chad maintains good relationships with foreign countries and unsteady relations with its regional neighbors. The next section of this case study will describe Chad's interaction with its neighbors, namely Libya, Sudan, and Nigeria.

Libya

In the mid-1970s, the Chad-Libya relationship began to deteriorate. The Libyan Army invaded the Aozou region in an effort to claim it as Libyan territory. During this period Libya consistently provided support to rebel movements inside Chad to overthrow the Chadian regime. A military coup eventually received overwhelming support from Libya to successfully overthrow the Chadian regime in 1981. The Libyan backed leader Mr. Goukouni, worked with Libyan leadership in order to bring unity between Chad and Libya.

The regime change resulted in outside assistance from France and the US to remove the Libyan backed leader Mr. Goukouni. In 1982, Mr. Goukouni left office and fighting between Chad and Libya continued over Libyan attempts to occupy the Aouzou strip, where an abundance of rich uranium deposits were located, according to Libya.

In 1990, the conflict continued, and Chad and Libya took the issue to the International Court of Justice. Ultimately, after several failed attempts to settle the dispute, the International Court of Justice ruled in favor of Chad, and Libyan forces slowly withdrew from the Aouzou strip (1994).[27] Eventually, Chad and Libya signed a treaty of friendship and cooperation between the two countries (April 4, 1994.)[28]

In the year 2000, although tension still remained between Chad and Libya, leaders of the respective nations worked together to build strong working relationships. However, a year later, in 2001 the good working relationship turned into a bitter relationship. Chadian President, Mr. Deby, accused Libya of supporting a rebel movement in Chad. After discussions and affirmation from the Libyan President that no Libyan forces would support a rebel movement in Chad, the relationship was once again in good standing. As a show of good faith, Chad made a public denunciation of sanctions against Libya.[29]

In 2002, Libya brokered a peace deal with rebels from northern Chad, officially ending the ongoing conflict in the region. The fighting has continued nonetheless.[30] Because of the north south division, political agendas, and neighboring Sudan refugee situation in Chad, various rebel groups continued to wage on-off rebellions against the Chadian government. In 2007, Libyan leaders brought Chadian leaders and rebel leaders to the table to broker a peace deal. Signed in Libya, the peace deal resulted in stopping a Chadian Army deployment. The parties also agreed to an immediate ceasefire, an amnesty for civil and military personnel, and the release of all prisoners.[31] The peace deal was also guaranteed by Libyan leadership and that assured all parties would adhere to the agreement.

Sudan

The countries developed social and religious ties, prior to Chad and Sudan gaining their independence. The relationship was vibrant in spite of disputes between the two countries. After Chad's independence in 1960 (four years after Sudan), southern leaders quickly took control with the support of France. As northerners began to rebel against the south's authority, Sudan became an important rear base for the north.

In the 1960s, political differences between the two countries were apparent and Chad's southern bias in leadership offended many Sudanese Muslims.[32] As a result, Sudan permitted northern Chadian rebels to train, organize, and create bases in Sudan. In 1966, the first armed rebellion was organized and launched from Sudan's Darfur Province. This marked the beginning of a conflict that consumed both countries for many years to come.

Although Sudan permitted Chadian rebels to launch attacks from the Darfur Province, relations between the countries remained affable on account of fearing Libyan involvement. Sudanese officials made an effort to convince Chadian government officials to allow rebels to play a role in government matters because of their talents. Before the talks concluded, relations between Chad and Sudan were strained because the Sudanese leadership developed closer ties with Libya.

As violence in Chad grew in the early 80s, rebellion in Sudan led to the Sudanese president overthrow (1983). Although the two countries were dealing with their own complex circumstances, the Chadian president, in1988 accused Sudan of giving Libyan troops permission to stage on the Chadian border. Additionally, Chad blamed Sudan of continuing to allow attacks against Chad to initiate in Sudan.

After a Chadian regime change in 1990, Chadian Sudanese relations began to improve.

Around the same time clashes in Sudan increased. Since the current Chadian regime had been loyal supporters of Sudan, the Sudanese rebels consistently asked for assistance but Chad denied all requests. Ultimately, Chadian armed forces deployed to fight against the Sudanese rebels inside the Darfur Province.

After a series of back and forth clashes a peace treaty was signed between the Sudanese government and Sudanese rebels, mediated by the president of Chad. Signed in the capital city of N'Djamena in 2004, the peace treaty led to the Chadian government's lose of credibility from the standpoint of the Sudanese government and rebels; additionally, the Chadian President was not successful in deterring those closest to him from supporting Sudanese rebels and Sudanese officials held that against him.[33]

The relationship between Chad and Sudan showed extreme strain by 2005 because of cross border issues. Chad blamed Sudan for permitting rebels to operate from Darfur who were accused of attacking Chadian citizens, killing people, and stealing cattle. Along with these concerns, Chad also faced the issue of refugees pouring in from Sudan from the Darfur province to escape violence. The influx of refugees resulted in overcrowded refugee camps.

In 2006, Chad blamed Sudan for supporting and supplying arms to rebels, who launched attacks in the capital city of N'Djamena and Mongo. Sudan, in turn, denied the charge and countered with blaming Chad for supporting anti-government groups operating in Darfur.

During this period the French envoy to the UN from France confirmed that rebels were active on the Chad-Sudan border. This resulted in further border clashes that fueled Chad and Sudan tension until 2009 when Sudan filed a complaint to the UN regarding Chad's violation of Sudan's sovereignty.

Nigeria

The Chad – Nigeria relationship has been plagued with conflict. Clashes between Chad and Nigeria date back to the 1970s when the two countries were at odds on account of plans for oil reserves around Lake Chad. Both countries were eager to settle the disagreement by establishing joint patrols and a commission that distinguished the boundary across the lake more clearly.[34] Despite the efforts to settle matters amicably, in the early 1980s, further disagreements surfaced when small islands from Lake Chad were identified. This complicated the relationship because it disturbed well established informal trade networks.

Nigerian instability in the north further complicated matters. Nigerian Islamic fundamentalism began to rise and resulted in violence throughout the 1980s.[35] The violence stemmed from religious clashes, and generally remained internal to Nigeria. Libyans arrested in Nigeria gained visibility from Nigerian police who accused the Libyans of penetrating through Chad. Although Chad received blame for allowing Libyans to penetrate Nigeria, Nigeria tried to form a stronger bond with Chad to receive economic benefits by growing regional trade relations.

Nigeria expelled several hundred thousand foreign workers, mostly from its oil industry, which faced drastic cuts as a result of declining world oil prices.[36] Many of the workers expelled were Chadian citizens; however, to maintain close ties both countries recognized the value of trade across their borders that lacked regulation.

In 1983, tension overshadowed the Chadian Nigerian relationship. Chadian troops conducted a series of attacks between April 18 and May 25 1983 on a Nigerian Army outpost.[37] These attacks resulted in nine Nigerian soldiers killed and 19 taken as prisoners. This conflict as rooted in the dispute regarding Lake Chad and other bordering islands thought to be rich in resources.

Nigerian government officials felt that Chad was a viable threat to its national interests and citizens due to the following:

a. The problem of fishing rights on the Lake Chad basin and the incessant harassment of Nigerian fishermen by Chadian soldiers and fishermen.

b. The perennial problem of boundary demarcation on the Lake Chad basin area.

c. Nigeria's diminishing interest in the Lake Chad basin in favor of the Chad basin development authority, which was demonstrated by the huge financial commitment by Nigeria of an estimated four hundred and ninety-eight million naira (N498, 000.000.00).

d. The expulsion of about 700,000 Chadians affected by the Nigerian deportation order of January 17, 1983.[38]

All of the aforementioned threats which Nigeria attributed to Chad simply relate to improperly defined boundaries.

The Chadian Civil War placed Nigerian security in a precarious position. As refugees fled Chad to avoid violence they settled in Nigeria and caused problems for Nigerian officials and police. Nigerian leaders supported a quick end to the Chadian Civil War because they felt the fighting, if not contained, would make its way into Nigeria. Due to the extreme build of power during the Chadian Civil War, Nigeria also viewed Chad as a major threat to Nigeria's security for fear of a quick Chadian military build-up in the face of future hostilities between the countries.

International Response

The international community supports widespread peace in Chad. Currently, solutions to Chad's internal and external problems, to include the proxy-war against Sudan are key interests. Due to the complexity of Chad's internal affairs, a majority of international efforts are primarily directed toward resolving cross-border issues. Without resolving border issues the region will remain prone to violence. If the international community fails to lay the foundation for a more inclusive and comprehensive strategy in Chad that targets the root causes of the conflict and engages all-actors into a peace process, lawlessness, banditry, and impunity will continue to ravage Chad and to impede progress in the region.[39]

United Nations

Resolution 1778 passed by the U.N. Security Council on September 25, 2007, approved the organization of a multinational force presence in Chad. In establishing the multinational presence the UN wished to:

(1) contribute to the protection of refugees, internally displaced persons (IDPs) and civilians in danger

(2) facilitate the provision of humanitarian assistance

(3) create favorable conditions for reconstruction and economic and social development.[40]

Resolution 1778 established a UN mission and a European Union (EU) military force under a single mandate.[41] Known as the U.N. Mission in the Central African Republic and Chad (MINURCAT), has the responsibility of training police forces and strengthening judicial systems. Additionally, MINURCAT has the task of working side by side with the Chadian

15

Army to emphasize the importance of keeping refugees, IDPs, and aid agencies safe. The EU force (EUFOR), has the task of providing security for citizens and also ensuring the safe and free movement of humanitarian personnel and assistance. EURFOR also has authority to use military force, while MINURCAT lacks the authority to use military force.

The international community is under that assumption that it is counter-productive to have two individual missions in Chad. Both missions tend to result in varying opinions and perceptions of Chadian citizens to include rebel groups. The statement in fact proved to be true. Some Chadian rebels see EURFOR as a "foreign occupation army," due to the presence of French military forces, which the rebels do not see as neutral. However, violence has been minimal and so has the French military force presence in the region.

In 2007, 3,700 EUFOR troops had their deployment orders delayed because of logistics and funding difficulties. Furthermore, additional delays plagued the mission in February 2008 when rebels advanced on N'Djamena. The force reached initial operating capacity, with almost half its full force deployed in March, and as of December 2008, 3,300 troops had deployed.[42] The late deployment of forces received great criticism from Chadian President Mr. Deby and aid groups who claimed EUFOR failed to protect them.

In March 2009, the EURFOR mandate expired and EUFOR transferred control to UN military forces. With a new mandate (Resolution 1861), MINURCAT received authorization to have a military component of 5,200 troops.[43] The 5,200 troop goal changed on account of the shortage of air assets used for troop transport. By the end of 2009, no more than 3,000 troops deployed, but the pace picked up significantly. In April 2010, force strength stood at nearly 3,500 troops. Although the pace of deployment picked up, the shortage of troops hindered MINURCAT's capacity to protect IDPs, refugees, and humanitarian staff.

Chadian officials appealed to the UN not to renew MINURCAT's military forces mandate. This was in part due to the sluggish tempo of troop deployments and planned infrastructure projects that were not on schedule. The government wanted to have the sole responsibility of protecting its citizens although it clearly did not have the capability. After dialogue between the UN and Chad, the Chadian government decided to keep the MINURCAT force and settled for a gradual drawdown and a transfer of authority to security forces in Chad. Also outlined in the mandate were the Chadian government's commitment to assume full responsibility for:

(1) ensuring the security and protection of civilians in danger, particularly refugees and IDPs

(2) facilitating the delivery of humanitarian aid and the free movement of humanitarian personnel by improving security in eastern Chad

(3) ensuring the security and freedom of movement of MINURCAT staff and United Nations and associated personnel.[44]

In 2012, working groups comprised of Chad and UN personnel monitor the situation in Chad. The working groups provide assessments on progress made by the government related to civilian protection, including the voluntary return and resettlement of IDPs, demilitarization of the camps, and improved domestic law enforcement capacity. U.N. reports point to a shortage of financial and human resources in the Chadian justice sector, a lack of basic court and prison infrastructure, among other shortcomings, in the east, which in turn hampers efforts to address the high level of criminality in the region.[45]

United States

US Chadian relations are amiable, as the US is the chief humanitarian donor to Chad providing over $700 million in assistance since 2004. The US continues to commit efforts to strengthen regional stability and security to promote Chad's progress and deter conflict in the region. Counterterrorist operations and trafficking of people, illicit materials, and other goods remain a US concern that US-Chadian cooperation attempts to prevent such activity in the region.

US intervention primarily focuses on protecting and investing in Chadian citizens and consistently encourages peaceful decrees for Chadian conflicts both internal and external. The US has done the following in support of protecting the Chadian citizens:

(1) Provided humanitarian assistance to eastern Chad totaling $187.2 million in relief programs: $133 million in food aid and $54.3 million in grants to United Nations agencies, international organizations, and nongovernmental organizations (NGOs) who carried out programs in health, education, water and sanitation, agriculture and food security, protection, and logistics

(2) Supported peacekeeping forces stationed in eastern Chad, assigned the task of protecting humanitarian workers and vulnerable populations, with $180.8 million in security assistance.[46]

The United States Agency for Aid and Development is a large proponent of US support to Chad in regards to investing in Chadian citizens. USAID is responsible for numerous programs in Chad that include Agriculture, health and nutrition, community capacity building, and general food distribution are some of the programs that are currently ongoing in Chad.

USAID efforts have yielded outstanding results. In fiscal year 2009, the following assistance was provided:

(1) 61 villages (2,076 participants, including 1,492 women) were provided water hygiene education and point-of-use water purification techniques

(2) 1,209 children under 5 years of age received Vitamin A

(3) 295 newborns received essential newborn care

(4) 52 Village Nutrition Educators were trained in nutrition basics

(5) 19 birth attendants from 10 villages were trained in monitoring pregnancies, detecting risk, and assisting women during childbirth

(6) 18 field agents were trained in the techniques of child growth monitoring, nutrition surveillance, and the administration of micronutrients

(7) 61 villages benefited from micronutrient distribution and growth monitoring sessions[47]

Overall, the US is committed to supporting Chad; however, due to the complex circumstances in Chad, if the US wants to see results, political and social problems must be at the forefront of US intervention. Unless a coordinated and comprehensive U.S. Government policy is established to address the internal drivers of conflict within Chad, the hard work of ending armed conflict and human rights violations will be undermined.[48]

Conclusion

According to the United Nations, political and security conditions in Chad remain unstable, and increasing the instability is the deterioration of the humanitarian circumstances that leave nearly 2 million Chadian citizens at the risk of hunger. In the western Sahelian region of the country, the World Food Program warns that an estimated 60% of households, some 1.6 million people, are currently food insecure.[49] This is an ongoing issue in the west, while Chadian citizens in the east deal with different circumstances.

In the east, the region remains prone to violence due to clashes between government forces and rebel factions. The violence has forced nearly 200,000 Chadian citizens to flee from their homes. Additional, refugees from neighboring Central African Republic (CAR) and Sudan's Darfur region have fled violence in their own countries and now live in refugee camps in the east and southern Chad according to the United Nations High Commissioner for Refugees (UNHCR).[50] As Chadian government forces lack personnel, attacks have increased. Since Chad agreed to a slow withdrawal of MINURCAT forces, local citizens doubt if Chadian forces are up to the challenge of providing security for the population.

The January 2010 agreement between Chad and Sudan has significantly improved relations between the two countries. There has been a cease to providing support to rebel groups and political progress is present in the form of democratic elections. There is still room for improvement for Chadian social, political, economic, and military matters. Also, regional relationships must continue to grow in order to bring stability back to the Sahel region

APPENDIX B: CHADIAN DEMOGRAPHICS

Population	**10,758,945 (July 2011 est.)**
Age structure	0-14 years: 46% (male 2,510,656/female 2,441,780) 15-64 years: 51% (male 2,531,896/female 2,960,406) 65 years and over: 2.9% (male 131,805/female 182,402) (2011 est.)
Median age	Total: 16.8 years male: 15.6 years female: 17.9 years (2011 est.)
Population growth rate	2.009% (2011 est.)
Birth rate	39.4 births/1,000 population (2011 est.)
Death rate	15.47 deaths/1,000 population (July 2011 est.)
Net migration rate	-3.84 migrant(s)/1,000 population (2011 est.)
Urbanization	Urban population: 28% of total population (2010) rate of urbanization: 4.6% annual rate of change (2010-15 est.)
Sex ratio	At birth: 1.04 male(s)/female under 15 years: 1.03 male(s)/female 15-64 years: 0.85 male(s)/female 65 years and over: 0.73 male(s)/female total population: 0.92 male(s)/female (2011 est.)
Infant mortality rate	Total: 95.31 deaths/1,000 live births male: 101.18 deaths/1,000 live births female: 89.22 deaths/1,000 live births (2011 est.)
Life expectancy at birth	Total population: 48.33 years male: 47.28 years female: 49.43 years (2011 est.)
Total fertility rate	5.05 children born/woman (2011 est.)
HIV/AIDS - adult prevalence rate	3.4% (2009 est.)
HIV/AIDS - people living with HIV/AIDS	210,000 (2009 est.)
HIV/AIDS - deaths	11,000 (2009 est.)
Major infectious diseases	degree of risk: very high food or waterborne diseases: bacterial and protozoal diarrhea, hepatitis A, and typhoid fever vectorborne disease: malaria water contact disease: schistosomiasis respiratory disease: meningococcal meningitis animal contact disease: rabies (2009)
Nationality	noun: Chadian(s) adjective: Chadian

Ethnic groups	Sara 27.7%, Arab 12.3%, Mayo-Kebbi 11.5%, Kanem-Bornou 9%, Ouaddai 8.7%, Hadjarai 6.7%, Tandjile 6.5%, Gorane 6.3%, Fitri-Batha 4.7%, other 6.4%, unknown 0.3% (1993 census)
Religions	Muslim 53.1%, Catholic 20.1%, Protestant 14.2%, animist 7.3%, other 0.5%, unknown 1.7%, atheist 3.1% (1993 census)
Languages	French (official), Arabic (official), Sara (in south), more than 120 different languages and dialects
Literacy	definition: age 15 and over can read and write French or Arabic total population: 25.7% male: 40.8% female: 12.8% (2000 est.)
School life expectancy (primary to tertiary education)	total: 7 years male: 9 years female: 5 years (2009)
Education expenditures	3.2% of GDP (2009)
Maternal mortality rate	1,200 deaths/100,000 live births (2008)
Children under the age of 5 years underweight	33.9% (2004)
Health expenditures	7% of GDP (2009)
Physicians density	0.04 physicians/1,000 population (2004)
Hospital bed density	0.43 beds/1,000 population (2005)

APPENDIX D: CHAD HISTORICAL TIMELINE

1883-93 - Sudanese adventurer Rabih al-Zubayr conquers the kingdoms of Ouadai, Baguirmi and Kanem-Bornu, situated in what is now Chad.

1900 - France defeats al-Zubayr's army.

1913 - French conquest of Chad completed; Chad becomes a colony within French Equatorial Africa.

1946 - Chad becomes a French overseas territory with its own territorial parliament and representation in the French National Assembly.

1960 - Chad becomes independent with a southern Christian, Francois - later Ngarta - Tombalbaye, as president.

1963 - The banning of political parties triggers violent opposition in the Muslim north, led by the Chadian National Liberation Front, or Frolinat.

1966 - Northern revolt develops into a fully-fledged guerrilla war.

1973 - French troops help put down the northern revolt, but Frolinat continues guerrilla operations throughout the 1970s and 1980s with the help of weapons supplied by Libya.

Libyan Intervention

1975 - Tombalbaye deposed and killed in coup led by another southern Christian, Felix Malloum.

1977 - Libya annexes the northern Chadian Aouzou strip.

1979 - Malloum forced to flee the country; a coalition government headed by a Muslim northerner, Goukouni Oueddei, assumes power.

1980 - Libya sends in troops to support Oueddei in his fight against the Army of the North, led by a former prime minister, Hissene Habre.

1981 - Libyan troops withdraw at Oueddei's request.

1982 - Habre seizes power. He is later accused of mass political killings during his rule.

1983 - The Organization of African Unity recognizes Habre's government, but Oueddei's forces continue resistance in the north with Libyan help.

1987 - The combined troops of Frolinat and the Chadian Government, with French and US assistance, force Libya out of the entire northern region apart from the Aouzou strip and parts of Tibesti.

First Democratic Elections

1990 - Habre toppled by former ally, Idriss Deby.

1993 - National democracy conference sets up a transitional government with Deby as interim president and calls for free elections within a year.

1994 - International Court of Justice rejects Libyan claims on Aouzou and rules that Chad had sovereignty over the strip.

1996 - Deby wins Chad's first multi-party presidential election.

1997 - Deby's Patriotic Salvation Movement triumphs on legislative elections.

1998 - The Movement for Democracy and Justice in Chad, led by Deby's former Defence Minister, Youssouf Togoimi, begins armed rebellion against the government.

2001 - Senegalese court rules that upholds ruling that former Chadian President Habre should not be made to stand trial in Senegal, where he is in exile. It decided that Senegal's courts do not have the jurisdiction to try Habre on torture charges during his eight years in power in Chad.

2001 May - Deby declared winner in controversial presidential poll.

Peace Deals

2002 January - Government and Movement for Democracy and Justice in Chad (MDJT) rebels sign Libyan-brokered peace deal intended to end three-year civil war.

2002 May - MDJT rebels and government forces clash in the far north; 64 are killed in the first outbreak of fighting since January's peace accord.

2003 October - Chad becomes an oil exporter with the opening of a pipeline connecting its oil fields with Cameroon.

2003 December - MDJT, government sign another peace accord. MDJT hardliners reject deal.

003 January - Government signs peace deal with National Resistance Army (ANR) rebels, active in the east.

2005 November - Former president, Hissene Habre, is arrested in Senegal over allegations of crimes against humanity.

Darfur Impact

2004 January-February - Thousands of Sudanese refugees arrive in Chad to escape fighting in Darfur region of western Sudan.

2004 April-May - Chadian troops clash with pro-Sudanese government militias as fighting in Sudan's Darfur region spills over the border.

2005 June - Voters back constitutional changes which allow the president to stand for a third term in 2006.

Rebel Battle

2006 April - Rebels seeking to oust President Deby battle government forces on the outskirts of the capital. Hundreds of people are killed. Chad cuts diplomatic ties with Sudan, accusing it of backing the rebels.

2006 May - President Deby is declared the winner of presidential elections. The main opposition parties boycott the poll.

2006 January-June - Thousands of refugees flee eastern areas as marauding Arab Janjaweed militia from Sudan's Darfur region penetrate deeper into Chad.

2006 July - Parliament approves the establishment of Chad's first state oil company, the Societe des Hydrocarbures du Tchad (SHT), which is expected to give Chad greater control over its energy assets.

2006 August - President Deby threatens to expel US energy giant Chevron and Malaysia's Petronas for failing to honor tax

2005 December - Rebels attack the town of Adre, near the Sudanese border. Chad accuses Sudan of being behind the incident.

2006 January - President Deby backs a law to reduce the amount of oil money spent on development. The move angers the World Bank, which suspends loans and orders the account used to collect oil revenues to be frozen.

2006 March - Government says an attempted military coup has been thwarted.

obligations, but relents after coming to an agreement with the companies.

2006 November - State of emergency imposed in eastern areas bordering Sudan's Darfur region after a spate of ethnic violence.

2006 December - Private newspapers stop publishing and several radio stations alter their programming to protest against state censorship under the state of emergency.

2007 February - UN refugee agency warns that violence against civilians in Chad could turn into a genocide.

2007 May - Chad and Sudan agree to stop conflict spilling across their borders but critics fear the agreement is unlikely to reduce the violence.

2007 August - Government, opposition agree to delay parliamentary elections by two years to 2009.

2007 September - UN Security Council authorizes a UN-European Union peacekeeping force to protect civilians from violence spilling over from Darfur in neighboring Sudan.

Emergency

2007 October - Emergency declared along eastern border and in the desert north.

Scandal as French charity tries to airlift a group of 100 "orphans" to Europe in what Chad describes as a smuggling operation.

2007 December - Six French aid workers are convicted of child-trafficking and sentenced to eight years' hard labour, but are then repatriated to serve their sentences at home.

2008 January - European Union approves a peacekeeping force for Chad to protect refugees from violence in Darfur.

2008 February - Rebel offensive reaches the streets of N'Djamena, coming close to the presidential palace; France sends extra troops.

Rebels are repulsed in fighting that leaves more than 100 dead.

2008 March - The presidents of Chad and Sudan sign an accord in Senegal aimed at halting five years of hostilities between the two countries

2008 May - Violence between Chadian and Sudanese militias flares up, leading to Sudan cutting diplomatic relations and Chad responding by closing its border and cutting economic ties.

2008 July - Security forces say they killed more than 70 followers of Muslim spiritual leader Ahmat Israel Bichara, who had threatened to launch a holy war, in fighting in southeast Chad.

2009 January - Eight rebel groups unite to form new rebel alliance, the Union of Resistance Forces (UFR), with Rally of Democratic Forces leader Timan Erdimi as its leader.

2009 March - European Union peacekeepers in eastern Chad hand over to a new, larger UN force known as Minurcat.

2009 May - UN Security Council condemns a major anti-government rebel offensive in the east.

2009 November - UN accuses Sudan of supporting URF rebels in Chad with arms and ammunition.

Six international aid groups, including the International Red Cross, suspend work in eastern Chad, citing risk of their staff being abducted or killed.

Rapprochement

2010 February - President Deby and his Sudanese counterpart, Omar al-Bashir, hold talks in Sudanese capital Khartoum, in their first meeting for six years; President al-Bashir says his country is ready for full normalisation of ties.

Chad and Sudan agree to deploy joint force to monitor situation along their shared border.

2010 March - Chad agrees to let UN peacekeeping force (Minurcat) to stay on for two months beyond the end of its mandate in mid-March, despite repeated criticism of its performance.

2010 April - Chad-Sudan border reopens seven years after Darfur conflict forced its closure.

2010 June - Voter registration closes ahead of parliamentary polls in November and presidential elections in April 2011.

2010 May - UN Security Council votes to withdraw Minurcat peacekeeping force from Chad and Central African Republic, deployed to protect displaced Chadians and refugees from Sudan's Darfur.

2010 July - Sudanese president Omar al-Bashir travels to Chad to attend a meeting of regional leaders - defying two warrants for his arrest issued by the International Criminal Court.

2010 September - Much of the country hit by flooding.

2010 October - Main political parties agree new timetable for postponed presidential and parliamentary polls.

Experts meet to discuss how to protect Lake Chad, which has shrunk dramatically over past 50 years.

50 Years of Independence

2011 January - Chad marks 50 years of independence from France.

2011 February - Parliamentary elections.

2011 April - Presidential election, boycotted by opposition. President Idriss Deby is declared winner.

2011 July - Following a UN appeal, Senegal suspends the planned repatriation of former Chadian President Hissene Habre to his homeland, where he has been sentenced to death for crimes against humanity while president from 1982-1990.

ENDNOTES

---

[1] Bessell, Sarah, and Kelly Campbell. *Toward Resolving Chad's Interlocking Conflicts*. Washington, D.C.: United States Institute of Peace, 2008, 11.

[2] Whitaker, Jennifer Seymour. *Africa and the United States: vital interests*. New York: New York University Press, 1978.

[3] Ploch, Lauren. *Instability and Humanitarian Conditions in Chad*. Washington, D.C.: Congressional Research Service, Library of Congress, 2010, 4.

[4] Bessell, Sarah, and Kelly Campbel, 14.

[5] "U.S. Department of State Background Note: Chad ." Infoplease: Encyclopedia, Almanac, Atlas, Biographies, Dictionary, Thesaurus. Free online reference, research & homework help. — Infoplease.com. http://www.infoplease.com/country/profiles/chad.html (accessed January 22, 2012).

[6] Collelo, Thomas. Chad A Country Study. Washington, D.C.: Federal Research Division, Library of Congress, 1988, 46.

[7] Collelo, 46.

[8] Collelo, 11

[9] Collelo, 140.

[10] Collelo,142.

[11] BBC News - Chad profile - Timeline."BBC - Homepage. http://www.bbc.co.uk/news/world-africa-13164690 (accessed February 7, 2012).

[12] Bekoe, Dorina. Stabilizing Chad: Security,Governance and Development Challenges. Washington D.C.: United States Institute of Peace, 2010, 2.

[13] Abubakar, Dauda. "SELECT LIBRARY." Credo Reference Home. http://www.credoreference.com/entry.do?ta=berkgpusnbn&uh=chad (accessed February 9, 2012).

[14] Abubakar, Dauda.

[15] University of Texas at Austin. "CEE PUBLICATIONS, 1991-2007." CENTER FOR ENERGY ECONOMICS. www.beg.utexas.edu/energyecon/publications.php (accessed February 11, 2012).

[16] Bekoe, 3.

[17] SIPRI Publications — www.sipri.org." Welcome to SIPRI — www.sipri.org. http://www.sipri.org/publications (accessed March 1, 2012).

[18] Collelo, Thomas 175.

[19] Collelo, Thomas, 175.

[20] Collelo, Thomas, 200.

[21] Collelo, Thomas, 201.

[22] " Republic of Chad", Background Notes on Countries of the World 2003/10495517, 20031108:EBSCOhost.-http://search.ebscohost.com/Login.aspx?r=50.4493758890323&svr=4&lang=en_us&x?direct=true&db=ECD&AN= 12036370

[23] "Chad ." Infoplease: Encyclopedia, Almanac, Atlas, Biographies, Dictionary, Thesaurus. Free online reference, research & homework help. — Infoplease.com. http://www.infoplease.com/country/profiles/chad.html (accessed February 13, 2012).

[24] Chad, Chad map, Chad flag." COUNTRIES OF THE WORLD, list of countries, list of asian countries, list of african countries, list of european countries, list of south american countries. http://www.enjoytravelling.net/chad/index.htm (accessed January 14, 2012).

[25] "Chad ." Infoplease: Encyclopedia, Almanac, Atlas, Biographies, Dictionary, Thesaurus. Free online reference, research & homework help. — Infoplease.com. http://www.infoplease.com/country/profiles/chad.html (accessed February 13, 2012).

[26] "CHAD: Foreign Relations." CountryWatch. search.countrywatch.com/cw_searchdocument.aspx?DocNumParam=51 (accessed February 13, 2012).

[27] CHAD: Foreign Relations." (accessed February 13, 2012).

[28] Foreign Relations Of Chad International Organization African." Business, Economy, Market Research, Finance, Income Tax Informations. http://www.economicexpert.com/a/Foreign:relations:of:Chad.html (accessed March 3, 2012).

[29] CHAD: Foreign Relations." (accessed February 13, 2012).

[30] CHAD: Foreign Relations." (accessed February 13, 2012).

[31] "BBC NEWS Africa Libya Seals Peace Deal for Chad." BBC News - Home. http://news.bbc.co.uk/2/hi/africa/7063093.stm (accessed February 13, 2012).

[32] Collelo,163.

[33] Tubiana, Jerome, and Emily Walmsley. The Chad-Sudan proxy war and the "darfurization" of Chad: myths and reality. Geneva: Small Arms Survey, 2008.

[34] Collelo,162

[35] Collelo, 162

[36] Collelo,162

[37] Omede, Adedoyin. Nigerias Relations with Her Neighbours. Ilorin: Department of Political Science, University of Ilorin, Ilorin, Kwara-State, Nigeria, 2006.

[38] Omede, 7.

[39] Tuckey, Beth. A Comprehensive and Inclusive Peace Process for Chad. Unknown: Africa Action, 2008, 3.

[40] Ploch, Lauren, 8.

[41] Ploch, Lauren. Instability in Chad. Ft. Belvoir: Defense Technical Information Center, 102008, 9.

[42] Ploch 5.

[43] Ploch, 9.

[44] Ploch, 9.

[45] Ploch, Lauren, 10.

[46] USAID. "Chad."U.S. Department of State. http://www.state.gov/r/pa/ei/bgn/37992.htm#relations (accessed March 1, 2012).

[47] USAID. "Chad."U.S. Department of State. http://www.state.gov/r/pa/ei/bgn/37992.htm#relations (accessed March 1, 2012).

[48] Tuckey,3.

[49] Ploch, 2.

[50] Ploch, 2.

BIBLIOGRAPHY

Abubakar, Dauda. "SELECT LIBRARY." Credo Reference Home.

> http://www.credoreference.com/entry.do?ta=berkgpusnbn&uh=chad (accessed February

> 9, 2012).

Arkhurst, Frederick S. *US Policy Toward Africa*. New York: Praeger [for] the Phelps

> StokesFund: 1975.

"BBC News - Chad Profile - Timeline." BBC - Homepage. http://www.bbc.co.uk/news/world

> africa-13164690 (accessed February 7, 2012).

"BBC News Africa Libya Seals Peace Deal For Chad." BBC News - Home.

> http://news.bbc.co.uk/2/hi/africa/7063093.stm (accessed February 13, 2012).

Bekoe, Dorina. *Stabilizing Chad: Security,Governance and Development Challenges*.

> Washington D.C.: United States Institute of Peace, 2010.

Bessell, Sarah, and Kelly Campbell. *Toward Resolving Chad's Interlocking Conflicts*.

> Washington, D.C. United States Institute of Peace, 2008.

"CHAD: Foreign Relations." CountryWatch.

> search.countrywatch.com/cw_searchdocument.aspx?DocNumParam=51 (accessed

> February 13,   2011).

"Chad ." Infoplease: Encyclopedia, Almanac, Atlas, Biographies, Dictionary, Thesaurus. Free

> online reference, research & homework help. — Infoplease.com.

> http://www.infoplease.com/country/profiles/chad.html (accessed February 13, 2012).

Collelo, Thomas. *Chad a Country Study*. Washington, D.C.: Federal Research Division, Library

> of Congress, 1988.

"Foreign Relations of Chad International Organization African." Business, Economy, Market Research, Finance, Income Tax Information. http://www.economicexpert.com/a/Foreign:relations:of:Chad.html (accessed March 3, 2012).

Henze, Paul B. *The United States and the Horn of Africa: History and Current Challenges*. Santa Monica, Calif. (1700 Main St., P.O. Box 2138, Santa Monica 90406-2138): Rand Corp., 1990.

Kitchen, Helen A.. *U.S. interests in Africa*. New York: Praeger ;, 1983.

Magyar, K. P.. *United States Interests and Policies in Africa: Transition to a New Era*. Houndmills, Basingstoke, Hampshire: Palgrave MacMillan, 2000.

Metz, Helen Chapin. *Egypt: A Country Study*. 5th ed. Washington, D.C.: The Division :, 1991.

Ofcansky, Thomas P., and LaVerle Bennette Berry. *Ethiopia: A Country Study*. 4th ed. Washington, D.C.: Federal Research Division, Library of Congress :, 1993.

Omede, Adedoyin. *Nigerias Relations with Her Neighbours*. Ilorin: Department of Political Science, University of Ilorin, Ilorin, Kwara-State, Nigeria, 2006.

Ploch, Lauren. *Africa Command U.S. Strategic Interests and the Role of the U.S. Military in Africa*. Washington, D.C.: Congressional Research Service, Library of Congress, 2007.

Ploch, Lauren. *Instability and Humanitarian Conditions in Chad*. Washington, D.C. Congressional Research Service, Library of Congress, 2010.

Ploch, Lauren. *Instability in Chad.* Ft. Belvoir: Defense Technical Information Center, 102008

Purkitt, Helen E.. African environmental and human security in the 21st century. Amherst, N.Y.: Cambria Press, 2010.

Rothchild, Donald S., and Edmond J. Keller. *Africa-US Relations: Strategic Encounters.* Boulder, Colo. Lynne Rienner, 2006.

"SIPRI Publications — www.sipri.org." Welcome to SIPRI — www.sipri.org. http://www.sipri.org/publications (accessed March 1, 2012).

Sullivan, Denis Joseph, and Kimberly Jones. *Global Security Watch--Egypt: A Reference Handbook.*Westport, Conn.: Praeger Security International, 2008.

Tubiana, Jerome, and Emily Walmsley. The Chad-Sudan Proxy War and the "Darfurization" Of Chad: Myths and Reality. Geneva: Small Arms Survey, 2008.

Tuckey, Beth. A Comprehensive and Inclusive Peace Process for Chad. unknown: Africa Action, 2008.

University of Texas at Austin. "CEE PUBLICATIONS, 1991-2007." Center for Energy Economics. www.beg.utexas.edu/energyecon/publications.php (accessed February 11, 2012).

USAID. "Chad." U.S. Department of State. http://www.state.gov/r/pa/ei/bgn/37992.htm#relations (accessed March 1, 2012).

Whitaker, Jennifer Seymour. *Africa and the United States: Vital Interests.* New York: New York University Press, 1978.